# WALK TALL

100 ways to live life to the fullest

This edition published in 2016
First published in 2008

Hardie Grant Books (Australia)
Ground Floor, Building 1
Richmond, Victoria 3121
www.hardiegrant.com.au

Hardie Grant Books (UK)
5th & 6th Floors
52–54 Southwark Street
London SE1 1UN
www.hardiegrant.co.uk

Cataloguing-in-Publication data is available from the National
Library of Australia.
Walk Tall: 100 ways to live life to the fullest
ISBN 978 1 74379 155 4

Cover design by Kinart
Text design and illustrations by Natalie Winter

Printed and bound in China by 1010 Printing International Limited

DR ANTHONY GUNN

# WALK TALL

100 ways to live life to the fullest

hardie grant books

Walk Tall …

'Look successful,
be successful.'

PROVERB

# Change your walk

Mismanaged fear and low self-esteem feed each other. High self-esteem, on the other hand, helps to put fear into perspective. High self-esteem is affected by three things:

Your THOUGHTS

Your EMOTIONS

Your ACTIONS.

Change one and you change all three. Starting from today, change just one of your actions and WALK TALL.

# Be selfish once a week

Many people take better care of their material possessions than they do of themselves. But if you lose your physical or mental health, no amount of money or cars, houses or fancy clothes will make up for it. Take time to look after yourself. Once a week do something for *you*. Lock yourself away from the world for an hour if you have to.

Look after yourself; you're worth spoiling.

# Make mistakes

Mistakes aren't bad. The fear of mistakes, though, will imprison you in your comfort zone. Instead of being scared of making a mistake, be scared of *not* making one, because without mistakes there is no growth. All great discoveries and accomplishments were made by making a mistake first.

'A person who never made a mistake
never tried anything new.'
ALBERT EINSTEIN

# Stress makes you dumb

When we are stressed our bodies release a chemical called cortisol to cope with the immediate threat. But when we remain stressed over a long period of time cortisol starts damaging brain cells, impacting our memory and ability to think. Result: we run around in circles believing that working harder will fix the problem, which only causes more damage. The good news is that brain cells damaged from stress can recover when the body is allowed to rest. This is why when we are feeling stressed, often doing less is best.

'Stress is basically a disconnection from the earth, a forgetting of the breath. Stress is an ignorant state. It believes that everything is an emergency. Nothing is that important. Just lie down.'

NATALIE GOLDBERG

# Is it multi-tasking or faulty-tasking?

Sit down on a chair and rotate your right foot in an anti-clockwise circle. Then with your right hand rotate it in a clockwise circle. Your foot will change direction. Why? It's a dilemma of the two brain halves: the left side of your brain controls the right side of your body, and the right brain the left side of your body. People get into similar troubles when multi-tasking while attempting something new and unfamiliar. Give yourself every chance of success by paying full attention to the boundary you are extending at the time.

'The brain is a lot like a computer. You may have several screens open on your desktop, but you're able to think about only one at a time.'

WILLIAM STIXRUD
*Neuropsychologist*

# Read with action

Most people read without ever applying what they've learned. As you read this book, apply your new-found knowledge to your life.

Don't just observe, take action — this is the key to walking tall.

'I hear and I forget.
I see and I remember.
I do and I understand.'

CONFUCIUS

# Fear keeps you sane

'When riding thirty-foot waves I use the saying, "Fear keeps you sane". This means that you don't go out there thinking that you are invincible. Instead, you go out there just a little afraid, knowing the ocean can take you whenever it's ready to. And life is like that.'

LAYNE BEACHLEY
*Seven-time world surfing champion*

# Look at the whole picture

Look at the two images below. What do you see? If you see a white triangle in the first image and a white sphere in the second, you've experienced a common human phenomenon. When we don't have all the information, we fill in the blanks so that we can create meaning.

We also jump to conclusions and try to fill in the blanks when we're judging what we can and cannot do. How many times have you looked at something new only to automatically fill in the blanks and assume you could never do it? That assumption is just the white triangle — it's not there unless you decide to draw it in. Assumptions about our abilities are often just illusions disguised as facts.

'Many people see what they expect to see instead of what is actually present in the situation.'

AARON T BECK

# Make ripples not waves

There's an old saying in the entertainment industry: 'It takes years to become an overnight success.' It's been shown time and time again that both patience and persistence are more important than talent alone.

'Success is incremental. It doesn't come in an avalanche. You know you are not going to move rocks; you are going to move small stones. And hopefully, if you move enough small stones or if you make enough ripples, you will create a tide. But it only starts with a ripple; the tide comes later.'

ALAN JONES

# Choose to be wrong

We don't like to be wrong. So, as strange as it sounds, if you think you can't do something, you'll unconsciously sabotage your efforts in order to be proven right. Increase your self-esteem by opening yourself up to the possibility that you're wrong about what you *cannot* do.

'The biggest obstacle to learning something new is the belief that you already know it.'

ZEN SAYING

# Tone your comfort zone

A common mistake people make is believing they only have to face a fear once for it to be conquered. Often a fear needs to be faced repeatedly to help develop the neural pathways in the brain to confidently perform the new action. These behaviours need to be exercised regularly to maintain your new-found courage. Each day, stretch your boundaries in small ways.

'We cannot become what we want to be by remaining what we are.'

MAX DEPREE

# Practise being a tosser

Hoarding things we no longer need or use often fuels anxiety and lowers confidence. Why? Because these objects act as a constant reminder of uncompleted tasks and make us feel that our lives aren't in order. It takes courage to let go of unused possessions, but your confidence will soar as a result. Starting today, what things can you sell, give to charity or toss out?

'Nothing is so fatiguing as the eternal hanging on of an uncompleted task.'

WILLIAM JAMES

Each
day
do
something
small
that
scares
you.

# Watch the crowd and then do the opposite

Humans naturally want to follow the crowd; it's an innate survival instinct. However, 'safety in numbers' often crushes individuality. There's no originality in a crowd. Watch what everyone else is doing and then do the opposite. That's where the riches in life are found. Go on, take that original idea you have and act on it. Especially if the crowd thinks it won't work.

'When you do the common things in life in an uncommon way, you will command the attention of the world.'

ANONYMOUS

# Write down your fears

Write your fears down on paper. This brings them out of hiding.

'Acknowledge your fear and bring
it out in the open.
Just doing this simple thing
will help you to be less afraid of it.'
Layne Beachley

# Accept compliments

Do you feel awkward when someone gives you a compliment? That's understandable, but rejecting a compliment insults the person who gave it — you are effectively criticising their judgement. Be gracious and say thank you. By accepting a compliment you are in turn giving a compliment, and it will also increase your self-esteem.

'A compliment is a gift, not to be thrown away carelessly, unless you want to hurt the giver.'

ELEANOR HAMILTON

# How big is your bowl?

A goldfish will only grow as big as the bowl you place it in. The moment you step out of your fishbowl — your comfort zone — your chance of growing increases. Why live in a fishbowl when there is a whole ocean out there to be explored?

'Never be afraid to try something new. Remember, amateurs built the ark, professionals built the *Titanic*.'

ANONYMOUS

# Learn to let go

Often the things you choose to leave out are just as important in shaping your life as the things you include. What is holding you back in life that you can let go of?

'It is not daily increase but daily decrease; hack away the unessential.'

BRUCE LEE

# Surf your discomfort

People will often go to great lengths to avoid feeling the discomfort associated with trying something new. The good news is that if you sit with your discomfort it will quickly decrease. Treat your discomfort like a wave and surf it. A wave is initially very strong, but loses its strength the longer you ride it.

'Any change, even a change for the better, is always accompanied by drawbacks and discomforts.'

ARNOLD BENNETT

# Chocolate can help fear

The secret everyone wants to hear: chocolate can help you practise surfing discomfort before you step out of your comfort zone. Take one small square of chocolate and place it on your tongue for two minutes with your eyes closed. Sounds easy! Here's the challenge: under no circumstances are you to react to the chocolate by swallowing, biting down, moving your mouth, jaw, neck or head. Remain still for the whole two minutes, surf the discomfort and watch it decrease. Give it a go and see how long you last.

'Strength is the capacity to break a chocolate bar into four pieces with your bare hands — and then eat just one of the pieces.'

JUDITH VIORST

# Break free

A baby elephant begins its training by having a chain tied around its ankle. At first the elephant fights against it, but in time learns that the chain can't be broken. At this point the trainer replaces the chain with a thin rope, and the elephant continues to assume that it can't break free. We, too, are often like that elephant, allowing ourselves to be held prisoner by string disguised as chains. Why? For many people, being trapped in a situation feels familiar and gives us a sense of security. We get used to our captivity. Freedom can feel unfamiliar and scary. For example, imagine being chained in debt for an expensive car you can't really afford. What would happen if you broke away from that chain; what would that freedom give you? What other chains might be holding you back in life?

'The secret of happiness is freedom. The secret of freedom is courage.'

THUCYDIDES

# Write to your skeletons

Relative to size, the strongest muscle in the body is the tongue. However, when it comes to talking about our issues, this mighty muscle often freezes. Bottling up past hurts can erode your confidence. Write down what's bothering you to help the brain process the issue. No-one else needs to read it, and you can destroy it once written. If at times the writing becomes difficult, leave it and come back later. This simple exercise will do wonders for your confidence. What skeletons can you clear out of your closet with pen and paper?

'There are thousands of causes for stress, and one antidote to stress is self-expression. That's what happens to me every day. My thoughts get off my chest, down my sleeves and onto my pad.'

GARSON KANIN

# The key to ~~success~~ failure

Humans are hardwired to fear negative comments from others. When our early ancestors were kicked out of their clans, it meant certain death. Thousands of years later, fear of rejection still dominates.

Not caring what other people think is unlikely; accepting and surfing the discomfort associated with not pleasing everyone is practical.

'I don't know what the key to success is, but the key to failure is trying to please everybody.'

BILL COSBY

# Fearlessness is an illusion

There is no such thing as a fearless person. Our brains are built to feel fear for our own protection. To say you don't feel fear is nothing short of saying that your brain is damaged.

'A person who has no fear in a particular area — maybe. A person who has no fear in all areas — impossible.'

STEVE VAN ZWIETEN

# 'Dedication ultimately proves better than ability.'

RAY WHEATLEY
*Vice-President of the International Boxing Federation*

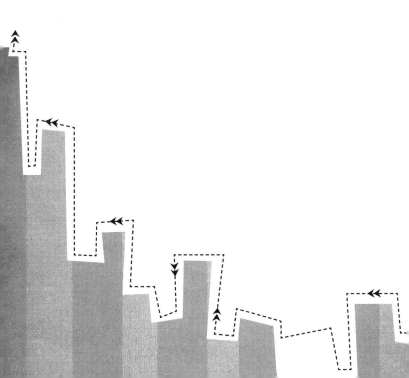

# Luck is a lottery

One way people gain a sense of control when dealing with fearful situations is to rely on luck. But luck is unpredictable and something over which we have no control. If luck does come your way, make the most of it, but to rely solely on luck when dealing with fear can be lethal. Instead, focus on controlling your own reaction.

'Success is a matter of luck, ask any failure.'

ANONYMOUS

# Overconfidence is overrated

One of the biggest dangers of all is being overconfident and blind to risks. Overconfidence can make you lose touch with your inbuilt protector — FEAR.

Make no mistake: focusing on the positives and being confident is good for you. But considering the risks keeps you alert to potential dangers and allows you to plan against them happening.

'Of course I get scared, especially when you think that in a fight, one punch can change your whole life forever. Thinking this helps me be ready at all times.'

KOSTYA TSZYU

# Create more tension

Whenever we are preparing to face a new situation, fear makes our bodies tense up, ready to fight or flight. To lower this tension, simply create more of it. Whenever you create tension in a muscle and then release this tension, the muscle has no choice but to relax. Briefly make the stress in particular parts of your body worse by tensing up. Make your hand into a tight fist and hold it for ten seconds. Then stop tensing and notice the difference in how your hand feels.

'Every action has an equal and opposite reaction.'
SIR ISAAC NEWTON

# Listen to people's actions

Many people are quick to give constructive criticism to others, but slow to apply it to their own lives. Consider the feedback but be careful of people whose actions conflict with the advice they are giving. They are often great at destroying confidence.

'Take my advice, because I'm not using it.'

ANONYMOUS

# Check your posture

How is your posture right now?
If you're slumped, straighten up.
Think tall and you'll walk tall.

# Become a Positive Pessimist

Positive Pessimism is preparing for the worst while expecting the best. Anticipate the worst and take measures to reduce the likelihood of it happening. This builds confidence so you can step out of your comfort zone.

A pessimist complains about the rain.
An optimist expects the rain to stop.
A Positive Pessimist carries an umbrella.

'You need to look at the "what ifs"
and act on them before they happen.'

PAUL BRIGGS

Learn to be a Positive Pessimist by using the following two questions:

1. What is the worst-case scenario? (Identifying the risks allows for a realistic assessment of them.)

2. Do you accept the worst-case scenario?
   - If an honest yes, then go for it.
   - If no, then what can you do to reduce the risks?
   - If no, and you cannot reduce the risks, then walk away.

If you cannot walk away, then accept the risks and focus on what you can control, like your own reaction to the situation.

'How was I able to fight with broken hands?
It wasn't that I had a bigger heart than anyone else,
I had just prepared myself to accept the worst.'
JEFF FENECH

# The drug of choice

Feeling down is notorious for leeching one's courage. Sometimes it's impossible to lift your low mood through positive thinking alone, without physical action. New research shows that exercise can be just as effective as taking anti-depressant medication (though do consult with your doctor if you are currently taking medication). Aim to exercise at least every second day for a minimum of 20 minutes, and notice your confidence and outlook on life brighten.

'A man's health can be judged by which he takes two at a time — pills or stairs.'

JOAN WELSH

# Everything is already broken

Buddhism teaches that as soon as you obtain any materialistic object, it has already started deteriorating. It's fine to look after material objects, though worshipping them is futile because they have a limited life. Many people treat their car, house, boat, etc. as a source of validation, as if it's an extension of themselves. Dependence on material objects is unstable — if your car gets dented, then so does your confidence. Aim to own an object, not have the object own you. Confidence from within will always be stronger than confidence based on external objects.

'If you see the glass not as half full or half empty, but as already broken, then if your glass ever breaks, just say, "Ah, there it goes," and calm down.'

RICHARD CARLSON

# Ease the pain

Often the pain from procrastination is just as bad as, and sometimes worse than, taking action. The sooner you face the discomfort, the sooner it will lessen. What have you been putting off doing? And are you prepared to live with the price of not following through on these actions?

'There is a price for everything we choose in life. You have to ask yourself, "Am I prepared to live with the price I have to pay?" '

WAYNE BENNETT

# Know the rewards

Think of something you have been avoiding. Ask yourself, 'What are the benefits of facing it?' Write them down. If you truly want these benefits, focusing on them will help give you the motivation to beat procrastination.

'You have to want to face a fear. Whether it be because of a strong desire to improve yourself or an interest in the task at hand — if you don't have this need, you'll prevent yourself from facing it every time.'

LAYNE BEACHLEY

'If someone says,
    "I CAN'T DO IT",
I ask them,
    "CAN'T do it
        or
DON'T WANT to do it?" '

JIM CASSIDY
*Winning jockey of two Melbourne Cups*

# A decision is better than no decision

Procrastination will trick you into thinking that making no decision is better than the wrong decision. By choosing no decision, you are still making a decision; you're just deciding to let procrastination win.

'When you have to make a choice and you don't make it, that itself is a choice.'

WILLIAM JAMES

# Look at the worst

Find the courage to look at the worst. Often in our attempt to avoid considering the worst, we make the worst seem darker than it really is.

'Being optimistic and ignoring the negatives is often what prevents you from handling fear. You need to look at the worst and say, "Well, it's not that bad, I can handle that, and if it happens, so be it." Then, if the worst does happen, you're not going to go into a total panic, because you've prepared yourself.'

GABY KENNARD

# 'Why' has to be stronger than 'How'

It's not *how* you leave a comfort zone, but *why* you leave it that can empower you.

'It doesn't matter what fear you are facing, before you do it, you have to ask yourself what your reason is for facing your fear in the first place.'

JOHNNY LEWIS

# Show the world

Show with your actions instead of your words. This
is how people will truly learn from you.

'A dog is not considered a good
dog because he is a good barker.
A man is not considered a good
man because he is a good talker.'

BUDDHA

# Face fear in front of your children

Children learn more through watching their parents than from what their parents say. Be a role model for your children by facing small everyday fears with them present. You will be teaching them not only how to manage fear, but also that it's normal to feel it in the first place.

'One mother teaches more than a hundred teachers.'

JEWISH PROVERB

# Ask **why** like a child

Children are experts at asking why. As adults, we've been so conditioned to keep up appearances that sometimes we forget to question. To walk tall you need to be able to ask 'Why?', like a child. If you feel you can't do something, ask yourself 'Why?' Once you have the answer, then question it again with 'Why?' Keep repeating this until you find the real source of your problem.

'A prudent question is one half of wisdom.'

FRANCIS BACON

# Friendly harmful advice

One of the most common and destructive pieces of advice a person can give is the platitude, 'Just remember, there are people worse off than you.' It is as if this will make you magically forget your concerns. It's important to maintain perspective in life but at the same time this advice implies that your fear is not justified, which in turn implies that you're simply complaining. Be aware of when harmful advice is disguised as helpful.

'Avoid pessimists — negativity is contagious.'

ANONYMOUS

# Small steps count

Procrastination tricks us into thinking that we have to
make a big step out of our comfort zones or nothing
at all. But your first step doesn't have to be huge. It can
be the tiniest of steps. Start small and you might feel
motivated to take a bigger step next time.

'You always have to know what your comfort
zone is and then be prepared to step out of it,
even if it's the smallest of steps.'

LAYNE BEACHLEY

# There will always be risks

To expect that there will be no risks when you're outside your comfort zone is unrealistic. Likewise, to wait until all risks have gone completely before stepping out of your comfort zone will be a lifelong wait. Risks can never be entirely eliminated. Accept them as a part of life, get to know them and then you can prevent them from occurring.

'It is of vital importance knowing what could go wrong. Otherwise you would not survive. I am always expecting a problem and try to anticipate it before it happens.'

RON TAYLOR

# Talk about death

Anxiety disorders impact at least one in ten people. Often at the core of this anxiety is an unconscious fear of dying. Many people believe they'll live forever and will never die, making death a taboo topic to discuss. Procrastinating, staying busy or taking crazy physical risks are ways of denying the fear of death. When one's immortality and limited time on this earth is honestly accepted, the courage to put things in perspective becomes easier. If you knew you had one week to live, what unfinished business would you take care of?

'Courage is living each day of your life like it's your last.'

UNKNOWN

# Try softer, not harder

Instead of trying harder not to make mistakes, ease up and *allow* yourself to make mistakes. The moment we allow ourselves to make a mistake it frees up our thinking to perform better because we are no longer focusing on what we shouldn't do, instead we are focusing on what we should do. What small comfort zone can you step out of to practise being open to making mistakes?

'The greatest mistake you can make in life is to be continually fearing you will make one.'

ELBERT HUBBARD

# Choose your competitions carefully

Who are you trying to compete with by keeping up appearances: neighbours, work colleagues, friends, family or even total strangers? Competition affects your judgement. Ask yourself, 'Are the competitions I'm choosing to compete in really worth it?'

'An archer competing for a clay vessel shoots effortlessly, his skill and concentration unimpeded. If the prize is changed to a brass ornament, his hands begin to shake. If it is changed to gold, he squints as if he were going blind. His abilities do not deteriorate, but his belief in them does, as he allows the supposed value of an external reward to cloud his vision.'

KEN FOX

# Excise your negative thoughts

The average person talks to themselves at more than 500 words per minute, of which over 70 per cent is negative. For the next five minutes keep track of what you are telling yourself. Note how these thoughts are making you feel. Go on, put down the book and do it now.

'Mind is everything;
what we think we become.'

BUDDHA

# Share your fear

There's nothing truer than the age-old saying that 'a problem shared is a problem halved'. If I could recommend only one practice to maintain your equilibrium, it would be talking with someone you trust. Who can you share your fear with today? Start by sharing a small fear. Pick up the phone, write a letter, type an email or talk to a trusted person face to face and share your fear.

'When competing, fear is a big factor for any athlete, and a good trainer helps them manage it. Getting others' support when managing fear is crucial.'

TONY O'LOUGHLIN

# All in the family

Your upbringing can be a big stumbling block in sharing your fears. If you were raised in an environment where talking about feelings was not the done thing, you may put up a barrier between yourself and others. By understanding your past, you'll be better positioned to take action and change the parts of yourself that are holding you back — namely, sharing your fear.

'The further back you look, the further forward you can see.'

WINSTON CHURCHILL

# Find yourself a fear friend

A fear friend is a trusted person you can share your fears with. A fear friend will support, but not rescue, you when fear is present. It's one thing to let someone help you carry your 'fear baggage' and quite another to allow them to be in full control of it. A Fear Friend will let you take ownership of your fear, but will be there as back-up if you need help.

'A friend is someone who understands your past, believes in your future and accepts you just the way you are.'

ANONYMOUS

# Read a little, often

No matter how busy you are, take time to read every day. Even if it's ten minutes before you go to sleep, read. Visit your local bookshop or library. The answer to a problem can often be found in a book.

'Books are the quietest and most constant of friends; they are the most accessible and wisest of counsellors, and the most patient of teachers.'

CHARLES W ELLIOT

What are your
thoughts at the
moment — positive
or negative?

THINK
TALL
AND
YOU'LL
WALK
TALL.

# Know when to walk away

Walk away from a fearful situation when you feel the risks outweigh the gains. This is different from procrastination, which entices you to stay in your comfort zone. Many people find it difficult to distinguish between the two and feel guilty or weak for walking away from a fearful situation. Remember, there is an important difference between not doing something that may harm you and not doing something that may strengthen you.

'He who knows when he can fight and when he cannot will be victorious.'

SUN TZU

# Tie up loose ends

Deal with incomplete or unnecessary things in your life. Clear out your wardrobe of old clothes; file incomplete paperwork. Unfinished business will only serve as reminders of failure.

'100 per cent of the shots you don't take don't go in.'

WAYNE GRETZKY

# Learn to 'live with it' instead of 'get over it'

As a psychologist, I regularly see the damaging effects that the 'get over it' mindset has on people who feel they must forget past failures or hurts. The common misconception is that you should be able to forget the pain from past setbacks by simply 'getting over it'.

You can't. We are not robots, we are humans with feelings. Instead, learn to live with past hurts by accepting them as part of you.

'Let yourself go with the disease, be with it, keep company with it — this is the way to be rid of it.'
BRUCE LEE

# Look for a fear role model

When you're preparing to face a past hurt or setback, model yourself on someone you consider courageous. This doesn't have to be someone you know personally. It could be a celebrity or even a fictional character. Often just watching or reading about how these people have learned to manage their fear can provide you with valuable support.

'If you are scared about trying something new, you can learn from other people who have been doing it longer than you.'

PAUL ISGRO

'You've got
to have
a reason
to be the
best because
talent alone
won't get
you there.'

JOHNNY LEWIS

*Trainer of three world boxing champions*

# Distort your distracting thought

Get to know your distracting thoughts in detail. Examine them from different angles, angles you may not have used before. Question the truthfulness of your unhelpful thoughts. One of the best ways to distort them is to deliberately focus on your unhelpful thoughts and observe how they behave. Give them more attention than they bargained for. This is the key to controlling them.

'The only reason some people get lost in thought is because it's unfamiliar territory.'

PAUL FIX

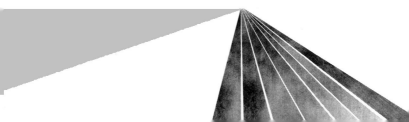

# The protester's picket line

Think of a distracting thought as a protester's picket line, blocking your way until their point of view is heard. If you ignore them or push them away, the protester becomes more determined. However, if you take the protester by the hand, sit them down and listen to their concerns, all that pent-up energy dissipates. Apply the same approach to distracting thoughts, listen to them carefully, but remember to question their accuracy and motives.

'Never interrupt your enemy
when he is making a mistake.'

NAPOLEON BONAPARTE

People are more pre-occupied with losing than winning.

Focus on success and you'll instantly separate yourself from the crowd.

# Imperfection still works

It deosn't mttaer in waht oredr the ltteers in a wrod are, the olny iprmoatnt tihng is taht the frist and lsat ltteers are in the rghit pclae. The rset can be a taotl mses and you can sitll raed it wouthit a porbelm. Tihngs dno't hvae to be pfrecet to sitll wrok.

'Courage is the power to let go of the familiar.'
RAYMOND LINDQUIST

# Courage is believing in yourself

A common misconception is that to believe in yourself you must be 100 per cent confident of success and, if you feel fear, you must have doubts. Reject this kind of thinking — we all feel fear. It doesn't mean we don't believe in ourselves. Believing in yourself is about knowing you can handle your discomfort, especially when it tries to influence you to run from a challenge.

'Courage is believing in yourself.'

NEVILLE KENNARD

Walk Tall …

'To plant a tree
is to believe
in tomorrow.'

ANONYMOUS

# Breathe easy

Incorrect breathing can lead to stress, ailments and panic attacks. Correct breathing is done from the base of your stomach and not from the tops of your lungs. For thirty seconds, breathe in and out as fast as you can. By the end of the thirty seconds you may feel light-headed or see stars, but these feelings of hyperventilation cannot hurt you. Now breathe from the pit of your stomach until you feel settled again.

Be aware of which style of breathing you use on a daily basis and aim for the one that will leave you feeling strong, not breathless.

'One way to break up any kind of tension is good deep breathing.'

BYRON NELSON

# Appreciate your own meal

Humans have an overriding urge to ignore what we have, and want what we don't have. When the waiter brings out a beautiful meal and places it in front of us, we might glance at our plate, but then look around the restaurant at what others are eating to see what we're missing out on. Instead, consider that the others are missing out on what *you* have.

'If you start focusing on what you have, and what you are grateful for, you will begin to see more.'

OPRAH WINFREY

# Think small to walk tall

To change bad habits in your life, first start with the smaller bad habits, which are the foundation for the bigger ones. Pull out the smaller bad habits and the larger ones will come crashing down like a house of cards.

'Train yourself to do the things you don't like to do in everyday life. Make yourself do it and it will become a habit for you to change bigger things in your life that scare you. This will teach you to be brave in other areas of your life.'

KOSTYA TSZYU

Here are some ideas of small habits you can change:

- Say hello to a neighbour or colleague at work you wouldn't normally greet.

- Wear something different from what you usually wear.

- Change what you eat for breakfast for a week.

- Take public transport to work for one day instead of driving.

- Be a passenger while your partner drives the car, or vice versa.

'Training is where you sort out all the problems like fear, in preparation for the real thing.'

WAYNE BENNETT

# Write down your successes

Our minds naturally focus on our shortcomings, forgetting our victories. Don't rely on your memory — write down your successes. That way when your motivation levels are down, you can read your past victories for an instant pick-me-up.

'People often say that motivation doesn't last. Well, neither does bathing — that's why we recommend it daily.'

ZIG ZIGLAR

# Rewarded behaviour gets repeated

All animals, humans included, will repeat a behaviour if they get rewarded for it. When you take a step out of your comfort zone, no matter how small, reward yourself. It could be with chocolate, a bubble bath or whatever you think is appropriate. Push yourself to do things outside your comfort zone and then make sure you're rewarded when you do.

'Celebrate what you want to see more of.'

TOM PETERS

# Get up ten minutes earlier

Are you always late for appointments or work? Even though the stress caused by running late is bad for you, it's also very addictive. To break this bad habit, you need to step out of your comfort zone and force yourself to get ready ten minutes earlier. Take small steps to break bigger habits.

'If something anticipated arrives too late it finds us numb, wrung out from waiting, and we feel — nothing at all. The best things arrive on time.'

DOROTHY GILMAN

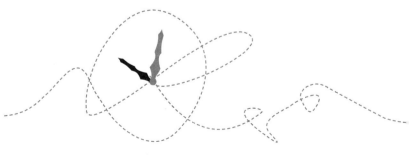

# Who's controlling your dreams?

Other people will often be quick to crush your ideas, telling you why they won't work. To agree and succumb to others' negativity is giving them permission to control your dreams. Remember, no one can take away ownership of your dreams unless you allow it. Who is in control of yours?

'People too weak to follow their own dreams will always find a way to discourage yours.'

ANONYMOUS

# Ask for directions

I once saw a bumper sticker that read, 'Real men don't ask for directions'. I wondered if that meant that real men were lost.

The majority of people approach a problem in denial. When faced with difficulty, so many of us refuse to stop and ask for help, and instead keep digging ourselves in deeper. If you find yourself in a hole, be brave and ask others for directions on how to get out.

'The most important thing to do if you find yourself in a hole is to stop digging.'

WARREN BUFFETT

# Whose fault is it really?

Responsibility is like the flu: most people are quick to pass it on. It's not easy to accept responsibility for our actions; we risk experiencing what we most fear — negative evaluation from others. But being honest in this way is extremely freeing and empowering. Try it.

'The one quality that all successful people have is the ability to take on responsibility.'

MICHAEL KORDA

# Listen to your intuition

We have two voices at work in our heads: the logical voice, which relies on proof and facts to make a decision, and intuition, which relies purely on a feeling or gut instinct. Intuition only says one thing without any justification. The logical voice gives multiple arguments. As soon as you have a feeling that cannot be backed up with logic, chances are it's your intuition.

'Don't ask me how the gut instinct works;
if I could explain it I'd be rich. Just listen to it.'

FRONT-LINE POLICE OFFICER

# Place feelings before facts

Humans are not machines. Facts may inform us, but feelings motivate us. Just think of all the cars bought for their image and not their practicality. The key to knowing your intuition is listening to your feelings.

'The intellect has little to do on the road to discovery. There comes a leap in consciousness, call it intuition or what you will, and the solution comes to you and you don't know how or why.'

ALBERT EINSTEIN

# Indecision often signals intuition

When you are having trouble deciding between two things, stop using logic. If it were that simple to think it through, you would have already done it. Instead, pay attention to the single command your intuition is telling you to do. Your intuition will only ever tell you what to do, not why you should do it.

'When I get a feeling that things aren't adding up or things aren't the way they should be, then I know it's my gut talking and I back off and wait for backup.'

FRONT-LINE POLICE OFFICER

# Control yourself to control your situation

The only thing you have full control over in this world is your own reaction. But when you're busy trying to control other people or things in a situation, you lose track of controlling yourself. To influence a situation, focus on controlling your own reaction — *think tall, feel tall, walk tall.*

'If you can control yourself on the inside and remain calm and focused, you have a greater chance of controlling what is happening outside.'

LAYNE BEACHLEY

# Names do hurt

'Sticks and stones will break my bones, but names will never hurt me.' If names didn't hurt, remembering such phrases wouldn't be necessary. Think back on your schooling. If you're like most people who've been bullied, the memories still cut deep years later. You're playing into a bully's hands by trying to ignore their mind games. Instead, expose the bully and bring their mind games out into the open.

'People will do whatever you let them get away with.'
MELISSA GUNN

# Dance with two left feet

For mind games to work, a bully needs you to cooperate and dance their dance. React differently from what a bully expects and it disrupts their normal thought patterns. If you don't follow their rules, the game won't work and they'll be forced to look for a new dance partner. One way of doing this is openly naming the bullying game they are playing instead of keeping quiet.

'Don't play the bully's game; do the opposite of what they expect and use the element of surprise or you'll get beaten every time.'

TONY WEHBEE

# Our greatest fear

What is our greatest fear? Answer: worrying what other people think of us. It rules everything we do, from the cars we drive, the houses we live in, the clothes we wear, our careers, even the way we do our hair. It's highly likely that the majority of your comfort zones will be influenced by social fear. You can't get rid of this deep-rooted fear; it's hardwired in our brains. Just know this fear is normal, accept it and then gradually face it by stepping out of your comfort zone in small steps. This will increase your social confidence.

'Nobody realises that some people expend tremendous energy merely to be normal.'

ALBERT CAMUS

# Optimism fluctuates

Research shows that when we are feeling fatigued we'll estimate our chances of successfully facing a future challenge as poor. In contrast, when we're feeling energised we will be far more optimistic about the thought of conquering that same challenge. Become aware of your own changing energy levels, and the natural cycles of peaks and troughs throughout the day. Pick your battles when your energy is on the rise.

'When our mood is low, even the most positive events become meaningless.'

DR ROBERT E THAYER

'Sometimes when you have a major calamity it helps you accelerate the process of breaking free of whatever it is you are trying to escape from.'

GABY KENNARD
*Record-breaking pilot*

# Welcome your fear

Fear can't be blocked out by sheer willpower no matter how much you try. This means it's not a lack of discipline on your part, or a sign of weakness. Any attempts to block out your fear are likely to be unsuccessful and, in the end, these failures will make you feel worse. Instead, welcome your fear as a natural protector designed to help.

'Insanity: doing the same thing over and over again and expecting different results.'

ALBERT EINSTEIN

# Your fears are unique

Comparing your fears with other people's fears will only set you up for failure. This is because your fears are based on your own life experiences, just as other people's fears are based on theirs. Our fingerprints are unique and so are our fears. Don't beat yourself up about them.

'Individuality is freedom lived.'

JOHN DOS PASSOS

# Just keep moving

We all want to start at the top instead of working our way up. It's human nature. However, many people fall into the trap of giving up if success doesn't come quickly enough. Success, in every area, comes to those who keep moving toward their goal instead of stopping at the first setback.

'Be not afraid of growing slowly,
be afraid of standing still.'

CHINESE PROVERB

'Success is getting
what you want.
Happiness is wanting
what you get.'

DAVE GARDNER
*Comedian and singer*

# Size is everything

Have you done something new that was absolutely terrifying, only to resolve that you would never allow yourself to be caught like that again? You may have faced your fear, but the cure ends up being worse than the complaint. Be wary of the supposedly classic cure for fear: facing it head-on without preparation. Face your fear in gradual and realistic baby steps. The size of your steps protects against having your confidence shattered.

'Don't take the bull by the horns, take him by the tail; then you can let go when you want to.'

JOSH BILLINGS

# Encourage fear to do its worst

Instead of trying to ignore your racing heart or trembling hands, encourage fear to do its worst. Try to make your hands shake harder or your heart beat faster. By doing so you are no longer fighting it — a battle you'll never win — and are instead accepting your fear. It's amazing how powerful this simple technique is at lowering your body's reaction to fear.

'Use fear on fear; you have to be scared when facing a new challenge because if you aren't scared, you will take unnecessary chances and won't get that rush you need to see you through.'

ROD WATERHOUSE

# Negative thoughts are normal

You're as likely to have positive thoughts all the time as you are to win the lottery. It is normal to experience negative thoughts when preparing to leave a comfort zone. Acknowledge your negative thoughts; allow them to be present without passing judgement or accepting them as truth, while continuing to walk tall toward your goal. This is how you will be free.

'It is the mark of an educated mind to be able to entertain a thought without accepting it.'

ARISTOTLE

# Prepare to lose

Sounds like a negative statement, right? WRONG!

A common misconception is that winners never think about losing. Often we attract that which we try to avoid, like losing. The moment you can accept the possibility of losing, you'll be free to focus all your attention on winning because you won't be hampered by trying to block out unwanted thoughts.

'The difference between a novice and a champion is this: the fear of losing is something a champion accepts.'

JEFF FENECH

# Things are best when worst

An old saying suggests that people are at their best when things are worst. When the chips are down, people forget about keeping up appearances and show their true colours in the form of weakness or strength. You have a choice in how you react. Choose to be at your best when things are worst and you'll stand out from the crowd.

'People are like stained-glass windows. They sparkle and shine when the sun is out, but when the darkness sets in, their beauty is revealed only if there is a light within.'

ELIZABETH KUBLER ROSS

# Even the Beatles were rejected

If you have had a new idea or invention rejected by others, then you've fallen victim to a very common human condition. We crave familiarity and will reject things that are new for fear of the unknown. The key is accepting this as a human condition and not as a personal insult. Be persistent. All great success stories, even the Beatles, were initially rejected by others.

'Those who dance are called insane
by those who don't hear the music.'

EDDIE VEDDER

# Watch successful people

Watch other people face a situation similar to the one that scares you. Modelling yourself on successful people in the area you want to succeed in is a powerful psychological tool for achieving success.

'Human beings, who are almost unique in having the ability to learn from the experience of others, are also remarkable for their apparent disinclination to do so.'

DOUGLAS ADAMS

# How do you attribute your setbacks?

Successful people attribute setbacks to external, situational factors. The defeatist mindset attributes setbacks to personal flaws in one's own character. Setbacks are vital in developing life skills. It's how you attribute the cause of setbacks which separates winners from losers.

'Smooth seas do not make for a skilful sailor.'

AFRICAN PROVERB

# What type of hat are you wearing?

The biggest factor that affects how people treat us is our self-concept — the way we see ourselves. It's a bit like a hat: it can show how we feel about ourselves and how we expect others to treat us. Recognise any of these hats?

THE SUBMISSIVE HAT: 'If I say anything it will only cause trouble.'

THE FAILURE HAT: 'I could never try that. I'd fail.'

THE BLUFFING HAT: 'Just act like everything is fine so no one will know I'm upset.'

What type of hat are you wearing?

'Low self-esteem is like driving through life with your hand-brake on.'

ANONYMOUS

# Treat your psychological wounds

Like a physical wound, untreated psychological wounds run the risk of becoming infected, contaminating your whole body. Use first-aid for your psychological wounds:

1. Acknowledge the wound. You're entitled to feel the way you do.
2. Accept the influence your pain is having on you and give the wound the care it needs.
3. Sit with the discomfort of the wound knowing time will heal it.

'We cannot be more sensitive to pleasure without being more sensitive to pain.'

ALAN WATTS

# Make fear your friend

Befriending fear is a way of taking control of the physical sensations it brings. Seeing fear only as a powerful ally is different from seeing it as a friend. When you see fear as a powerful ally you are accepting only its positive attributes. When you see fear as a friend, you are accepting it for what it is, warts and all. When fear is unconditionally accepted, you can harness its power much more easily.

'I have found the best way to manage the physical effects of fear is to treat them as normal.'

STEVE VAN ZWIETEN

# Think tall.
# Feel tall.
# Walk tall.

# About the author

Dr Anthony Gunn is a psychologist specialising in treating fears and phobias. He regularly speaks to sporting and social clubs, schools and professional institutions about fear and how to deal with it.

His other publications include *Swing High: Life Lessons from Childhood*, *Raising Confident Happy Children: 40 tips for helping your child succeed* and *Get Happy: Lessons in Lasting Happiness*.

For more info go to: www.anthonygunn.com

Sept/16